WORLD OF
MAMMALS

# BATS

WITHDRAWN

**By Sophie Lockwood**

*Content Adviser: Barbara E. Brown, Scientific Associate, Mammal Division, Field Museum of Chicago*

THE CHILD'S WORLD®, MANKATO, MINNESOTA

**Bats**

Published in the United States of America by The Child's World®
1980 Lookout Drive • Mankato, MN 56003-1705
800-599-READ • www.childsworld.com

## Acknowledgements:

The Child's World®: Mary Berendes, Publishing Director

The Creative Spark: Mary Francis, Project Director; Wendy Mead, Editor; Deborah Goodsite, Photo Researcher

The Design Lab: Kathleen Petelinsek, Designer and Production Artist

## Photos:

Cover: Joe McDonald/Animals Animals—Earth Scenes; frontispiece and page 4: Sean Kane/iStockphoto.com; half title: Hazlan Abdul Hakim/iStockphoto.com

Interior: Alamy: 14 (blickwinkel), 5 center left and 22 (Visual&Written SL), 26 (The Natural History Museum); AP Photo: 35 (Rob Griffith); iStockphoto.com: 5 top left and 10 (Kevin Smith), 5 bottom left and 36 (Michael Westhoff); Minden Pictures: 19 (Stephen Dalton), 28 (Pete Oxford), 5 bottom right and 31 (Claus Meyer); Peter Arnold, Inc.: 9 (S.J. Krasemann); Photolibrary Group: 5 top right and 13; Photo Researchers, Inc.: 21, 25 (Dr. Merlin D. Tuttle/Bat Conservation International); Visuals Unlimited: 16 (Bill Beatty).

## Library of Congress Cataloging-in-Publication Data

Lockwood, Sophie.
  Bats / by Sophie Lockwood.
      p. cm.—(The world of mammals)
  Includes index.
  ISBN 978-1-59296-926-5 (library bound : alk. paper)
  1. Bats—Juvenile literature. I. Title. II. Series.
  QL737.C5L63 2008
  599.4—dc22                           2007013565

# TABLE OF CONTENTS

## Chapter One

# A Whir of Wings

The sky over Bracken Cave in Central Texas is fading from bright blue to the coral, pink, and purple of sunset. Listen carefully. From the cave comes a flutter of wings. First a dozen bats emerge from the cave's entrance. Soon hundreds and thousands more follow. As they soar higher, they fill the sky with inky black splotches.

Within minutes, the flutter becomes a whir and then a roar as millions of Mexican free-tailed bats spiral into the sky. Great tornado-shaped columns rise up 3,000 meters (9,800 feet).

Between dusk and dawn, Bracken Cave's bat colony—consisting of around 20 million bats—feasts on 181 metric tons (200 U.S. tons) of flying insects. Nearly 90 percent of the meal consists of moths, but hungry Mexican free-tailed bats are not picky eaters. They happily munch on ground beetles, leaf chafers, weevils, leaf beetles, flying ants, water boatmen, green blowflies, and leafhoppers.

**Did You Know?**
Entering a cave where an endangered bat species roosts can end in a trip to court and a fine up to $7,500 under the Endangered Species Act.

Range of the
Mexican
Free-Tailed Bat

CANADA

U.S.A.

Bracken Cave

MEXICO          Gulf of Mexico

Atlantic
Ocean

Pacific
Ocean

This map shows the range of the Mexican free-tailed bat.

The bats roost in Bracken Cave from spring through early fall. These hungry **insectivores** devour from 6,000 to 18,000 metric tons of bugs yearly. That's a lot of bugs! Since the moths the bats eat would produce larvae that attack corn and cotton crops, these bats help Texas agriculture. They are the most effective **pesticide** available—with no side effects from poisoning the soil.

## FREE-TAILED BATS

The Mexican free-tailed bat—sometimes referred to as the Brazilian free-tailed bat—is one of more than one hundred species of free-tailed bats worldwide. These bats live in the southwestern United States, Mexico, Central America, the Caribbean islands, Chile, and Argentina. They are medium-sized, measuring about 9 centimeters (about 3.5 inches) long and weighing 15 grams (0.5 ounces). Free-tailed bats are easy to recognize. A large portion of their tail extends beyond the body.

Free-tailed bats roost in cool, dark caves or buildings. These bats adapt well to any environment with room to roost. In Austin, Texas, nearly one million free-tailed bats have formed a colony under the Congress Avenue Bridge. At a roost, the bats huddle in dense clusters.

Hanging from their roosts, the bats pass liquid and solid waste. At times, the bats raise their bodies to pass **urine** or **feces.** Sometimes, a bat allows urine to trickle through its fur before dropping. The strong-smelling urine helps get rid of body lice. A thick coating of guano—bat dung—quickly builds up on the cave floor. The guano produces ammonia, which makes crawling around in bat caves dangerous

*These are just a few of the millions of Mexican free-tailed bats that live in Bracken Cave.*

### Did You Know?

Bats are the only mammals that can actually fly. They have true wings and can swoop and collect prey mid-flight. With a strong tailwind, bats may fly at speeds up to 95 kilometers per hour (60 miles per hour).

for humans. While hazardous to humans, guano is great for growing plants—it is a wonderful fertilizer.

*A group of bats emerges from Bracken Cave.*

## SAVE THE BAT CAVE!

For more than ten thousand years, bats have come to Bracken Cave each spring. In recent years, Bat Conservation International has purchased 280 hectares (692 acres) of land around Bracken Cave. This bat habitat is safe, but much of the world's bat population faces habitat loss or disturbance.

Habitats are lost in several ways. Nearby rivers are dammed, creating man-made lakes that flood natural caves. Housing developments are built near bat-rich caves, and their residents foolishly kill the bats. At times, humans invade the caves and cause many bat deaths without realizing the harm they are causing.

Some bats **hibernate** (more about this later), and any disturbance during that time can lead to their death. They have only enough food reserves in their bodies to survive the hibernation period. If disturbed, the bats use up valuable energy that cannot be replaced during the time when food is scarce. When bats are disturbed during hibernation, they often die of **starvation.** Bat caves are for bats, and humans should stay away!

### Did You Know?

Bat watching is great entertainment. These caves provide the best places to watch bats emerge:

- Blowing Wind Cave and Hambrick Cave (Alabama)
- Point Reyes National Seashore (California)
- Bandelier National Monument (New Mexico)
- Carlsbad Caverns (New Mexico)
- Nickajack Cave (Tennessee)
- Bracken Cave and Eckert James River Bat Cave (Texas)

## Chapter Two

# Creatures of the Night

It is past midnight—blackness covers every tree, bush, and building. A little brown bat swoops through the sky, homes in on its prey, and ZAP! In a split second, another mosquito becomes bat dinner.

Bats are creatures of the night, and they fly safely through the darkness with the help of **echolocation.** This is the same process used by whales, dolphins, porpoises, and cave swiftlets. It is the way submarines find their way through deep seas.

Compared to bat echolocation, submarine **sonar** is weak. A submarine can locate other subs, whales, and large rock formations by bouncing sound waves off a hard substance. Measuring the time it takes for the echo to return allows the people in

**Did You Know?**
Bats clean themselves the same way cats do—they lick their fur clean.

*Bats, such as the greater horseshoe bat shown here, fly in search of food.*

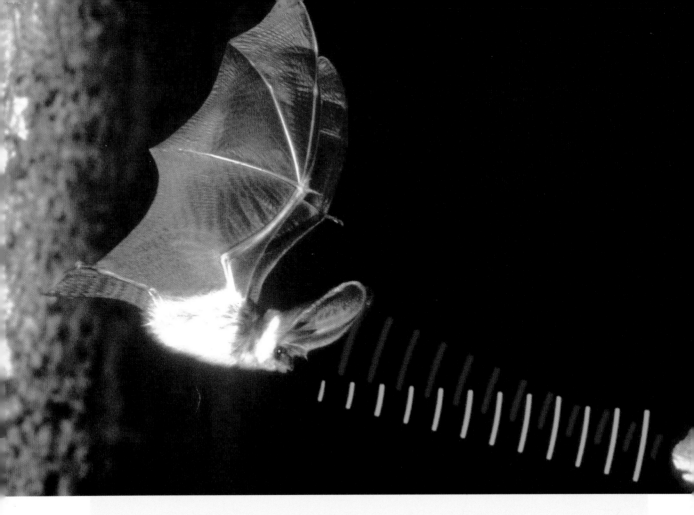

the sub to determine the distance to an object. Bat echolocation is a billion times more effective than submarine sonar. Bats can identify barriers as thin as a human hair. Not all bats have echolocation abilities. Some do not need it, but those bats that eat flying insects have it—and use it!

Here's how echolocation works. The bat emits sounds too high pitched for humans to hear. The sounds bounce off

**Did You Know?**
The saying "blind as a bat" makes absolutely no sense. Bats may have small eyes, but they see quite well.

*This illustration shows how a long-eared bat uses sound to find its prey.*

objects in the distance, and the bat hears the echo. From that echo, the bat can tell the size, shape, and distance of the object. It can distinguish a flower from a moth. In darkness, echo-location allows bats to "see" everything but color.

Several types of moths, lacewings, crickets, and mantids have sensitive hearing that lets them hear bat sounds. This excellent hearing allows them to avoid bats on the prowl. However, some bats have evolved ways to overcome the cleverness of flying insects. Spotted bats, for example, use low-frequency signals that are below the hearing ability of these insects. Other bats stop emitting sound when they get close to their prey. Without hearing a sound, insects cannot avoid the bats, and the bats catch a tasty meal.

## BAT WINGS

All bats can fly, but not all bats fly equally well. Small bats that feed on insects are quick, agile flyers because they need to be. It would be impossible to catch a darting mosquito with clumsy flight skills. Bats that feed on fruit, flowers, and nectar do not need terrific flying skills. A ripe mango does not zip through the air to avoid capture.

Bat wings are arms with the same basic bone structure as a human arm. Human arms have a long upper and two

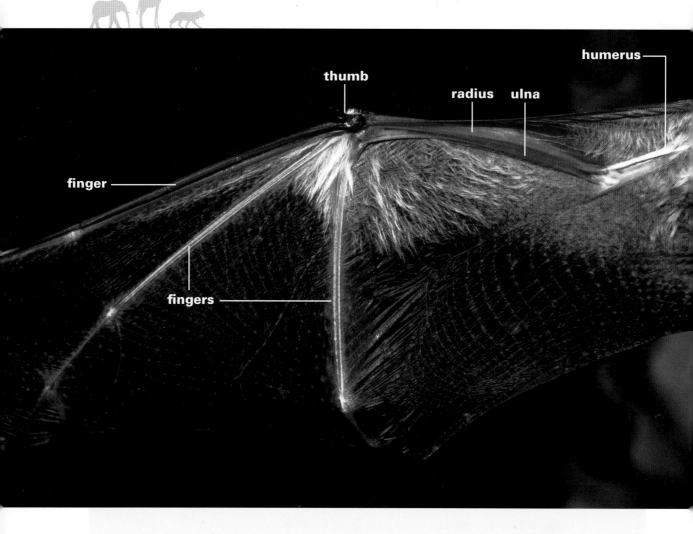

**thumb**

**radius** **ulna**

**humerus**

**finger**

**fingers**

forearm bones, the **humerus,** the **radius,** and the **ulna.**
Bat arms have a very short humerus, the bone closest to the
body. The radius and ulna form a joined bone that is twice
as long as the humerus. Human hands have a thumb and
four fingers. So do bat hands. The thumb is like a hook
halfway down the wing. The fingers are very long compared

*A close-up of a red bat shows its arm bones.*

to the bat's body, and the bones are flat. A thin, leathery skin called membrane stretches from the bat's trunk to the digits, creating a weblike wing. Bat wings consist only of bones and membrane which stretches over the entire wing and attaches to the body. The wings are much lighter than birds' wings.

## WHAT'S FOR DINNER?

Roughly 70 percent of bats eat insects, spiders, or scorpions. Bugs provide protein and fats. Moths offer the fat that bats need to hibernate. Tops on the standard bat menu are moths, mosquitoes, flies, beetles, cockroaches, crickets, katydids, and night-flying ants. While most bats prefer to get dinner on the wing, the pallid bat feeds on the ground. It scours the undergrowth for crickets, grasshoppers, and beetles.

Several bat species go after larger prey, such as toads, minnows, and even small bats. The fish-eating bat (*Myotis vivesi*) swoops down to catch minnows, much like a bald eagle catches trout. It has long feet with really long claws on its toes that help it grab small fish near the water's surface. Skilled fishing bats may capture thirty or more small fish a night. They can be

### Did You Know?

Bats are menu items for many Southeast Asians and Pacific Islanders. The Chamorro people of Guam, Australian Aborigines, and Indonesian natives eat big bats called flying foxes. These bats are hunted for food and sold in meat markets. They are part of the family Pteropodidae (TER-oh-po-did-ay), which contains more than 170 species.

found on the islands in the Sea of Cortez and in Baja California.

Most larger bats, like flying foxes, are fruit eaters. They only eat overripe fruit and, in fact, do not eat the fruit at all. They chew the pulp and suck the juice, then spit the pulp and seeds out. In tropical rain forests, bats are considered a **keystone species** because they play a crucial role in keeping the rain forest ecosystem healthy. Bats spread plant seeds and pollinate flowers. For example, Africa's baobab tree depends on bats to pollinate its flowers. The bats drink the flower nectar, and the tree thrives. Baobabs feed and house many animal species, and bats make sure the baobabs flourish.

Despite rumors to the contrary, only three types of bats suck blood. None come from Transylvania or have any connection to Dracula. Vampire bats live in Central and South America. One species does drink mammal blood. But it is perfectly happy sucking blood from cattle, not people. The other two species prefer bird blood and are not interested in the human variety.

So have no fear. The bat sleeping upside down in the attic does not drink human blood. If anything, the sight of *you* will scare the wits out of the bat.

*The species name for the common vampire bat is* Desmodus rotundus.

## Chapter Three

# Bat Habits

In Australia, a camp of gray-headed flying foxes sways gently in the breeze. They are roosting high in a stand of eucalyptus. They can be heard chirping and chattering some distance from the grove—and smelled from even farther. Bats roost in caves, cliff sides, and tree branches. They also roost in church steeples, on the underside of giant banana leaves, and in narrow slits in stalks of bamboo. A bat's home is wherever it hangs itself.

Bats spend much of their lives upside down. The place they do this hanging around is called a roost. Most bats have a day roost—a home base—and temporary night roosts for resting while hunting.

Upside-down sleeping may not suit humans, but bat bodies are designed specifically for sleeping head down. They have special valves in their arteries to keep blood from pooling in their heads. They cling to surfaces with special claws or pads on their feet. Bats have even developed a flight pattern that allows them to spread their wings and right their bodies quickly.

## MIGRATION AND HIBERNATION

Winter is coming, and for many bats that live in a **temperate** climate, it is time to **migrate.** Many bats migrate to escape the cold and the resulting lack of food, but some choose to hibernate. Bats remain loyal to their favorite places. They usually return to the same cave in a warmer climate to hibernate each year. Very little is known about bat migration. Some bats seem to follow the same paths as birds heading south. Others follow paths of their

*A mother Gambian epauletted fruit bat travels with her baby at night.*

own. It is possible that bats travel a set route each year, looking for specific landmarks along the way.

When the bats arrive at their winter quarters, it is time to mate. Like many animal species, the males put on a show to attract a female. The female is either impressed or not. Some male bats sing for their ladies. Others perform fancy flying tricks. Male

**Did You Know?**
Jamaican fruit-eating bats (*Artibeus jamaicensis*) form harems of up to fourteen females, with one male that protects them. This male mates with all the females to produce young. These bats have a soft, velvety coat and smell like perfumed soap. Despite their name, they can be found in other places besides Jamaica. They live from Central America to Brazil and in the Caribbean islands.

*Like many species of epauletted fruit bats, this Walberg's epauletted fruit bat lives in Africa.*

epauletted bats (part of the **genus** *Epomophorus*) sing and flash the fluffs of white fur on their shoulders. Crested bats create a display by making the hair on their heads stand on end.

Bat hibernation is a carefully timed event. Bats feed heavily to build body stores of fat before hibernating. When the bat enters hibernation, its **metabolism** slows down. Body temperature drops, and the bat rarely moves. Breathing slows, as does its heartbeat. Depending on size and species, bats hibernate for three to six months or longer. Ideally, a bat goes into hibernation as its most common foodstuff goes out of season and wakes up when a good-sized meal is available again.

## REPRODUCTION AND CHILDCARE

After migrating bats reach the end of their journey, the females become pregnant. All through the winter, **sperm** lies inactive in a hibernating female's body. Spring comes, bats awaken, and the sperm becomes active. This process is called **delayed implantation.** Females that do not hibernate usually mate in the spring.

Females settle together in a maternity ward of sorts. Pregnancies can last from forty days to ten months, depending on the type of bat, and infants are born alive. An infant

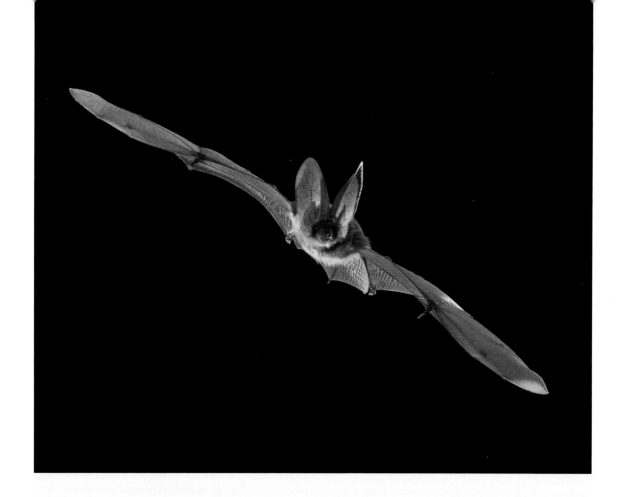

In the air, bats face a few determined hunters. Great horned owls are excellent night hunters and capture bats that are resting in temporary night roosts. Even more dangerous is the peregrine falcon. Falcons fly at remarkable speeds and can pluck flying bats from the sky.

The bats' greatest enemy, however, is human. Some humans fear bats and react to that fear by killing them. In the past one hundred years, humans have killed millions of bats without realizing that bats are essential members of our living world.

*Bats, such as this long-eared bat, can fly faster than many predators—but not all of them.*

## Chapter Four

# A Family of Bats

Bats live just about everywhere in the world. They can be found in all of the temperate and tropical regions. The only places you won't find bats are the Arctic and Antarctic. Flying foxes and other fruit eaters prefer tropical forests where plenty of fruit and flowers grow throughout the year. In rain forests, bats make up about one-fourth of all mammals.

Microchiroptera and Megachiroptera are the two main categories of bats. *Chiroptera* (keer-OP-tuhr-uh) comes from the Greek words for "hand wing." *Micro* (small) and *mega* (large) help define the type of bat, but even those labels are confusing. They imply that all microchiroptera are small, all megachiroptera are large, but that is not true. Microchiroptera weigh anywhere from 1.5 grams (0.05 ounces) to 200 grams (7 ounces). Megachiroptera weights range from 13 grams (0.5 ounces) to 1,500 grams (52 ounces) for large flying

foxes. The length of a bat's head and body can range from 25 to 406 millimeters (1 to 16 inches).

### FLYING FOXES

Flying foxes get their name from their faces. They look very much like small foxes with wings. As bats go, flying foxes are species giants. There are fifty-seven flying fox species, and they live in such exotic places as Tahiti, Samoa, and Fiji.

It would be hard to miss a camp of flying foxes—they shriek and chatter to each other, and the smell—pheww! When they are hanging around, flying foxes get rid of lice and other pests by grooming each other. Flying foxes eat fruit, but some species are known to eat flowers or drink nectar. Their long, slender tongues allow them to lap sweet nectar from deep, trumpet-shaped blossoms.

*A Madagascar flying fox soars in a special reserve on the African island of Madagascar.*

## VESPER BATS

Vesper bats comprise the largest bat family, known as Vespertilionidae (VEHS-pur-tih-lee-on-ih-dee), which has more than 330 known species. Vesper, or evening, bats cannot easily be grouped by habits, habitats, or appearance. They range from 4 grams (0.14 ounces) to 50 grams (1.8 ounces) in weight, and may be any color: brown, reddish, black, yellow, gray, or tan. Vesper bats roost in caves, trees, buildings, or anywhere quiet. They are hairy or not hairy. Most are insect eaters, but some eat fish. Some migrate while others stay in a stable home range. Some hibernate, but others do not. They have between twenty-six and thirty-eight teeth.

Scientists have found that labeling vesper bats is nearly impossible and definitely frustrating. They have come up with a handful of subfamilies, but even the bats in the subfamilies have major differences. For example, some pipistrelles are poor flyers, fluttering around like butterflies, but that is not true of all pipistrelles. *Myotis* bats live in caves, except for the ones that do not.

In North America, one common member of the vesper bat family is the big brown bat. Yes, that is their real name, although they have a long scientific name, too (*Eptesicus fuscus*). Big brown bats are a farmer's best friends. A colony

of 150 big brown bats can consume enough adult cucumber beetles in a summer to prevent egg laying that would result in 33 million larvae. Cucumber beetle larvae are serious corn pests, and 33 million could cause severe crop damage.

## NEW WORLD LEAF-NOSED BATS

Although the vesper bat family is larger, the most diverse bat family is the New World leaf-nosed bats, with more than 140 species. Found only in North, Central, and South America, leaf-nosed bats come in a variety of sizes, live in a variety of habitats, and have a variety of habits.

Most leaf-nosed bats eat a full menu of insects—flying, crawling, and burrowing. Some have branched out to add frogs, birds, mice, and small lizards to their menus. Still others drink only flower nectar; a few eat only fruit. True vampire bats, part of the leaf-nosed bat family, dine only on blood.

Leaf-nosed bats roost in odd places. Tent-making bats (*Uroderma bilobatum*) turn the underside of a banana leaf into a home. Dark, abandoned mine

**Would You Believe?**
The smallest bat in the world is the Kitti's hog-nosed bat (*Craseonycteris thonglongyai*), also known as the bumblebee bat, which is 30 to 44 millimeters (1.17 inches) long and weighs 2.2 grams (0.07 ounces). It is found in Thailand and Myanmar.

*This leaf-nosed bat lives in the South American country of Brazil.*

**Did You Know?**

Bats can communicate through scent and sound. Scent tells the males when females are ready to mate. It helps mothers find their babies. Infant bats appear to have distinctive voices. Among millions of young in a nursery, a mother finds her own baby by its smell and voice.

shafts and tunnels make nice shelters for California leaf-nosed bats (*Macrotus californicus*). Other family members roost in caves, in cactuses, in cracks in rocks, or under clay roof tiles. These adaptable bats can live in cloud forests, on mountains, and in deserts.

The California leaf-nosed bat has a remarkable skill. It hovers like a helicopter. This allows the bat to pluck insects from plants without having to land. Its flying ability matches that of most hummingbirds, and its hearing is so sharp, it detects the footsteps of crickets and the crunches of feeding caterpillars. Another interesting fact about the California leaf-nosed bat is that it has never been seen drinking water.

# Chapter Five

# The Past, Present, and Future

For more than 50 million years, bats have flown the night skies. At one time, they were as common as pigeons in a city park. Unfortunately for bats, some humans see bats as a threat and act to get rid of that threat. It is only within the past fifty years that humans have learned enough about bats to appreciate their economic and environmental value.

It was only after scientists began studying bats that people realized that they make excellent neighbors. Bats work while humans sleep, ridding the area of insects and spiders. Many insects can hear bat sounds from 30 meters (98 feet) away and avoid coming into a bat's territory.

In Chautauqua, New York, lectures and classes are held in the open air each summer. For decades, the Chautauqua Institution has encouraged bats to roost in the area. The result is an insect-free environment where visitors never have to worry about being bitten by mosquitoes or spraying themselves with bug repellant.

Insect control is one positive aspect of encouraging bats. Another is farm profits. More than 300 plant species in tropical forests depend on bats for pollination and spreading seeds. These plants provide 450 different products sold worldwide. Products include 110 food and drink items, 72 medicines, timber and bark, dyes, animal foods, and fuel. A number of fruit, nut, and spice trees also depend on bats for pollination, including bananas, cloves, cashew nuts, peaches, and avocados. If you drink cocoa, eat bananas, or make balsa wood model airplanes, you should thank a bat.

## CONSERVATION

Of the forty-five bat species in North America, six appear on the endangered species list. These species include the gray bat, Indiana bat, Ozark big-eared bat, Virginia big-eared bat, lesser long-nosed bat, and Mexican long-nosed bat. These and other bat species are in danger from loss of habitat, direct killing, being hunted as human food, and the use of pesticides.

The legal protection of bats, their habitats, or both will help bat species survive. Bat Conservation International

**Did You Know?**
Are bats deadly? It is safer to put up a bat house than it is to plant flowers. Blooms attract bees, and more people die each year from bee stings than suffer bat-related deaths.

(BCI) leads the way toward helping bats survive through a number of programs. They provide plans for building and using bat houses and monitor bat conservation projects around the world. A major part of BCI efforts is educating the public about the value of bats. They have an "adopt-a-bat" program, but readily point out that bats are a "look-but-do-not-touch" animal species.

*A volunteer feeds fruit bats that were injured in a cyclone in Australia.*

*Putting up bat houses is one way you can help these amazing flying mammals.*

Bat World Sanctuary in Texas offers rescue and rehabilitation to injured and abandoned bats. They raise bat orphans and provide medical treatment for wounded bats. The group also provides a home for bats that cannot be returned to the wild.

## WHAT CAN YOU DO?

To help bats, learn as much as possible about them and their habitats. Follow these simple do's and don'ts. Never disturb a bat habitat—not even for a quick look. Do not touch a bat lying on the ground—it may be sick, and it is a wild animal. If you do find such a bat, call your local animal control or health department.

Think about building a bat house for your backyard. Bats will eventually find their new home and move in. A family in Lee County, Florida, put up a one-room bat house in June 2000. For several years, the house, mounted on a pole 5 meters (16 feet) above ground, attracted small colonies of Mexican free-tailed bats. In 2003, a different group of larger bats moved in. These bats were Wagner's bonneted bats—Florida's rarest and largest bats. This Florida family has made a difference for this bat species. You can, too. For bats, success and survival depend on very small human efforts.

# Glossary

**delayed implantation** (dee-LAYD im-plan-TAY-shun) a process in which a female mates but does not become pregnant with young until much later

**echolocation** (ek-oh-loh-KAY-shun) the ability to determine the location of other objects by sending out sound waves

**feces** (FEE-seez) the solid waste of an animal

**genus** (JEE-nuss) the major subdivision of a family or subfamily in the classification of organisms, usually consisting of more than one species

**hibernate** (HY-bur-nayt) the act of sleeping through the winter months

**humerus** (HYOO-mer-uhs) the bone in the upper part of the arm

**insectivores** (in-SEK-tuh-vorz) animals that eat insects

**keystone species** (KEE-stohn SPEE-sheez) a species that other plants and animals depend on for survival

**metabolism** (muh-TAB-uh-lizm) the chemical changes and processes through which the body uses nutrients

**migrate** (MY-grayt) to move from one location to another, usually in search of food

**pesticide** (PESS-tuh-syd) a chemical compound used to kill insects and other small pests

**predators** (PREH-duh-turz) animals that hunt and kill other animals for food

**radius** (RAY-dee-uss) a bone in the lower part of the arm

**sonar** (SOH-nar) a system that determines the position of unseen underwater objects by sending out sound waves and measuring the time it takes for the echo to return

**sperm** (SPURM) male reproductive cells used to fertilize a female's eggs

**starvation** (star-VAY-shun) the act of dying from lack of food

**temperate** (TEM-per-ut) having weather that is not extremely hot or extremely cold

**ulna** (ULL-nuh) a bone in the lower part of the arm

**urine** (YUR-in) liquid animal waste

# For More Information

## Watch It

*Bat Talk—The Secret Language of Mexican Free-tailed Bats*, DVD (Austin, TX: French and Lollar, 2000)

*Kids Discover Bats*, DVD (Austin, TX: Big Kids Productions, 2005)

*The Secret World of Bats*, DVD (Austin, TX: Bat Conservation International, 2005)

## Read It

Editors of TIME for Kids. *Time for Kids: Bats!* New York: HarperCollins, 2005.

Markle, Sandra. *Outside and Inside Bats*. New York: Walker & Company, 2004.

Merrick, Patrick. *Vampire Bats*. Chanhassen, MN: The Child's World, 2001.

Vogel, Julia. *Bats—Our Wild World*. Minnetonka, MN: NorthWord Press, 2007.

Williams, Kim, Rob Mies, Donald Stokes, and Lillian Stokes. *Stoke's Beginner's Guide to Bats*. Boston: Little, Brown & Company, 2002.

Wood, Linda C. and Deane Rink. *Zoobooks: Bats*. Poway, CA: Wildlife Education, Ltd., 2001.

## Look It Up

Visit our Web page for lots of links about bats:
*http://www.childsworld.com/links*

Note to Parents, Teachers, and Librarians: We routinely verify our Web links to make sure they are safe, active sites—so encourage your readers to check them out!

## The Animal Kingdom
## Where Do Bats Fit In?

**Kingdom:** Animalia

**Phylum:** Chordata
(animals with backbones)

**Class:** Mammalia

**Order:** Chiroptera

**Suborders:**
Microchiroptera
Megachiroptera

# Index

## About the Author

Sophie Lockwood is a former teacher and a longtime writer. She writes textbooks, newspaper articles, and magazine articles. Sophie enjoys writing about animals and their habits. The most interesting part of her research, Sophie says, is learning how scientists apply their knowledge to save endangered species. She lives with her husband in the foothills of the Blue Ridge Mountains.